D1602016

LEHI'S DREAM

LEHI BEHELD THE FRUIT

LEHI'S DREAM

ART BY

JAMES C. CHRISTENSEN

TEXT BY ROBERT L. MILLET

DESERET
BOOK

Salt Lake City, Utah

Hold to the Rod, the Iron Rod, on page 66, © James C. Christensen, courtesy of The Greenwich Workshop®, Inc. For more information about artwork by James Christensen, visit www.GreenwichWorkshop.com.

Library of Congress Cataloging-in-Publication Data
Millet, Robert L., author.
    Lehi's dream / Robert L. Millet ; illustrated by James C. Christensen.
        pages cm
    Includes bibliographical references.
    Summary: Robert L. Millet explains the context and symbolism of Lehi's dream from the Book of Mormon, accompanied by new artwork commissioned for the book by James C. Christensen.
        ISBN 978-1-60641-225-1 (hardbound : alk. paper)
    1. Lehi's dream—Criticism, interpretation, etc. 2. Lehi's dream—Art. 3. Tree of life—Symbolic aspects. 4. Symbolism in the Book of Mormon. 5. The Church of Jesus Christ of Latter-day Saints—Doctrines. I. Christensen, James, 1942– illustrator. II. Title.
        BX8627.M54 2011
        289.3'22—dc23   2011029535

Printed in Canada
Friesens, Altona, Manitoba, Canada

10 9 8 7 6 5 4 3 2 1

THE SCRIPTURES ARE RICH WITH STORIES. THE HISTORY OF THE ANCIENTS, AS INDIVIDUALS AND GROUPS, GIVE US MANY INSIGHTS INTO THE NATURE OF MAN AND GOD'S RELATIONSHIP TO HIS CHILDREN.

—JAMES C. CHRISTENSEN

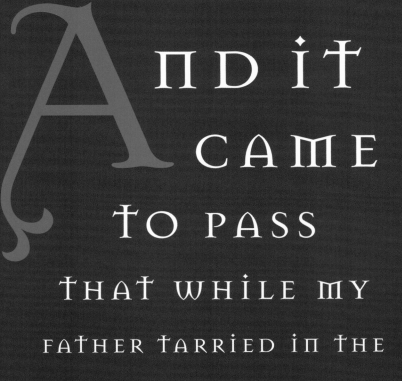

AND IT CAME TO PASS THAT WHILE MY FATHER TARRIED IN THE WILDERNESS HE SPAKE UNTO US, SAYING:

BEHOLD, I HAVE dreamed a dream; or, in other words, I have seen a vision.

And behold, because of the thing which I have seen, I have reason to rejoice in the Lord because of Nephi and also of Sam; for I have reason to suppose that they, and also many of their seed, will be saved.

But behold, Laman and Lemuel, I fear exceedingly because of you; for behold, methought I saw in my dream, a dark and dreary wilderness.

1 Nephi 8:2–4

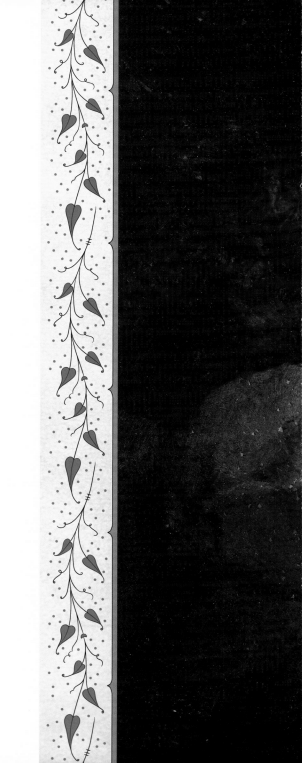

THE BOOK OF Mormon story begins in Jerusalem in the first year of the reign of Zedekiah, king of Judah, in about 600 B.C. (1 Nephi 1:4). It is a time of great strife and unrest: Jerusalem, literally but ironically the "city of peace," is under siege, and Nebuchadnezzar, king of Babylon, has positioned his armies outside the city, biding his time before undertaking a complete overthrow of Judah's capital. Holy prophets, chosen spokesmen for God, roam the streets and sound a warning voice (1 Nephi 1:4). We cannot tell from the record how and to what extent such prophetic personalities as Obadiah, Daniel, Habakkuk, Ezekiel, Jeremiah, and Lehi interacted with one another, including who held the keys or directing power of the ministry, but we do know that God's house is a house of order, not a house of confusion (D&C 132:8). We also know that it is a time of gross wickedness—men and women have hardened their hearts, stiffened their necks, and broken their covenants; the people of Israel—called out from the Gentile nations and charged by Deity to be a light to the world—are living far beneath their spiritual privileges, well below the divine standard Moses received at Sinai to be "a kingdom of priests, and an holy nation" (Exodus 19:6).

It is at this dark day that God determines that he will separate out a body of people, lead them out of wickedness, and bring them to a land "choice above all other lands" (1 Nephi 2:20).

It all begins with a family. God calls upon a faithful Israelite to take his family, leave behind their affluence, escape into the wilderness, and prepare themselves for relocation to the promised land. Lehi's little colony makes its way into the desert (presumably down the western coast of the Arabian peninsula) and for almost a decade travels in a south-southeastern direction until they set sail for America. This undertaking would have been arduous at best, even had all of the colony been supportive of Lehi and his sons Nephi and Sam. But they were not: Laman and Lemuel, the older brothers, possessed by their possessions, murmur constantly. They "did murmur against their father . . . because they knew not the dealings of that God who had created them" (1 Nephi 2:12).

Those in the Lehite colony are given repeated

opportunities to demonstrate their faith in God. Not long after leaving the holy city, Lehi's sons are asked to return to Jerusalem to obtain a scriptural record known as the brass plates, a sacred collection of prophecies from the time of the fall of Adam and Eve down to and including the words of Jeremiah, a prophet contemporaneous with Lehi. As usual, the elder brothers murmur, while Nephi, chosen by God as Lehi's prophetic successor, declares: "I will go and do the things which the Lord hath commanded, for I know that the Lord giveth no commandments unto the children of men, save he shall prepare a way for them that they may accomplish the thing which he commandeth them" (1 Nephi 3:7). Nephi's words are a perfect demonstration of the kind of faith that leads to life and salvation: *I will go and do . . . for I know.* Jesus Christ himself will, some six centuries later, proclaim the formula for faith—do, then know (John 7:16–17; compare Ether 12:6).

With all of this as a dramatic backdrop, having gathered his family and "seeds of every kind" (1 Nephi 8:1), Lehi announces: "Behold, I have dreamed a dream; or, in other words, I have seen a vision" (1 Nephi 8:2). It is a divinely given dream, a dream that is also a vision, a message from heaven. It is poignantly personal to Lehi and his wife Sariah (1 Nephi 8:3–4), but also remarkably relevant to all humankind; it represents and embodies every man's quest for the good life, every woman's search for happiness, and the challenges we confront as we press through temptation toward eternal life. It is at once a capsule summary of the Book of Mormon story, a distillation of a tragic epic that plays itself out again and again, and at the same time, a pattern prophecy and a stark reminder for all nations, all villages, all families: God will not be mocked, and people ignore the counsel of his prophetic spokesmen at their own peril. Indeed, stark warning is sounded repeatedly: "Inasmuch as ye shall keep my commandments ye shall prosper in the land; but inasmuch as ye will not keep my commandments ye shall be cut off from my presence" (2 Nephi 1:20).

Aпd it came to pass that I saw a man, and he was dressed in a white robe; and he came and stood before me.

And it came to pass that he spake unto me, and bade me follow him.

And it came to pass that as I followed him I beheld myself that I was in a dark and dreary waste.

And after I had traveled for the space of many hours in darkness, I began to pray unto the Lord that he would have mercy on me, according to the multitude of his tender mercies.

1 Nephi 8:5–8

IN THE BOOK of Job, Elihu declared: "For God speaketh once, yea twice, yet man perceiveth it not. In a dream, in a vision of the night, when deep sleep falleth upon men, in slumberings upon the bed; then he openeth the ears of men, and sealeth their instruction" (Job 33:14–16). Ponder for a moment on how critical dreams/visions were for such persons as Jacob (Genesis 28:12–16), Joseph of Egypt (Genesis 37, 40, 41), Daniel (Daniel 2), Joseph the husband of Mary (Matthew 1:19–25; 2:19–21), the wise men (Matthew 2:12), and Peter (Acts 10). When the physical body has yielded to a needed rest, occasionally the Spirit of God begins to work upon the mind and heart of man. The distractions of the world and the preoccupations of the flesh are set aside, and Spirit is allowed to commune with spirit. The children of God may be instructed, comforted, chastened, warned, encouraged, or fortified in the faith. It may be during these special times that answers to lingering questions come, when disembodied loved ones who have long since slept communicate with their mortal kin.

Inspired dreams, to some extent like most other dreams, may be systematic, formulaic, or intuitive. And of course such divine communications are often symbolic—they point the participant (or, in our case, the reader) beyond the obvious and the literal to a grander, richer reality. Lehi sees "a dark and dreary wilderness" (1 Nephi 8:4), meaning a barren desert. Walking alone in the desert is frightening enough in broad daylight, but some of us can only begin to imagine how horrifying it would be to be traveling alone, in the desert at night, in a "dark and dreary" desert. *Dreary* brings to mind such words as *dismal*, *gloomy*, even *sorrowful*. The loneliness would be almost overwhelming. Feelings of hopelessness and despair would abound. Suddenly and thankfully Lehi sees another person—a man adorned in a white robe, who bids Lehi to follow him. As he does so, Lehi notes: "I beheld myself that I was in a dark and dreary waste" (1 Nephi 8:7). That is, Lehi finds himself traveling in desolate and uncultivated terrain for many hours, at which point he begins to plead with God for mercy, "according to the multitude of his tender mercies" (1 Nephi 8:8).

One of the words used in the Book of Mormon

most often to describe a person's fallen condition is the word *lost*. A lost person is very anxious about their present condition, very much aware that they are not where they need to be or ought to be. They know they need to go somewhere, but where? Some lost persons, in an effort to relieve the anxiety they feel, choose a course and pursue it feverishly, although there is anything but certitude in their soul as to the correctness of the course they are pursuing. And what is it they need most? They need a guide. In his dream Lehi may well have felt an ounce of relief as he sees the man clothed in a white robe. It is another human being, a treasured commodity when dreary

Tree of life, decorated border, from Siphnos, Cyclades

solitude is the alternative. And then the man beckons Lehi to follow him: surely the man knows where they are, where they need to go, and what path to pursue. Then, after traveling for many hours in darkness, Lehi begins to pour out his heart in prayer to Almighty God for relief, for rescue.

Because we live in a fallen world, every one of us begins the path to Christ and eternal life in darkness. We try it on our own for a season but soon discover that no amount of grit and willpower, no amount of personal discipline or behavior modification will bring us peace and fulfillment. We need help. Oh, how we need help! Since faith comes by hearing the word of God as it is preached by the spirit of prophecy and revelation (Romans 10:17),[1] a gracious Lord sends his authorized servants to point the way home. They teach and they testify. They warn and they exhort. They speak of the need for a complete conversion, a total rebirth, and they call us to repentance. Realizing our plight, acknowledging our impure and spiritually uncultivated condition, we cry out to our Father in heaven, in the name of his Son, for forgiveness and recovery. We turn to the only true source there is for peace and contentment in a noisy and confused world—we turn to God.

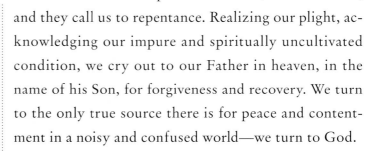

AND IT CAME to pass after I had prayed unto the Lord I beheld a large and spacious field.

And it came to pass that I beheld a tree, whose fruit was desirable to make one happy.

1 Nephi 8:9–10

EACH OF US comes into the kingdom in the broad way. We bring our talents, our gifts, our dispositions with us. At that point our world is like a spacious field—expansive, open, a vast number of lifestyles available for the taking. But it will not be that way for long. Discipleship is all about Christian discipline of the kind and quality that promotes righteous living. To fully accept Jesus Christ as Savior is to receive him as the Lord of our lives, to agree to the conditions of his covenant, to begin to comply with the guidelines established by his Church and kingdom. In the words of the apostle Paul, "If we live in the Spirit, let us also walk in the Spirit" (Galatians 5:25). In the parlance of our day, "If we talk the talk of Christianity, we really ought to walk the walk."

Genuine conversion is more than an expression of belief in the truth of the gospel. True faith is always manifest in faithfulness. James, the brother of the Lord, wrote: "Faith, if it hath not works, is dead, being alone. Yea, a man may say, Thou hast faith, and I have works: shew me thy faith without thy works, and I will shew thee my faith by my works. Thou believest that there is one God; thou doest well: the devils also believe, and tremble. But wilt thou know, O vain man, that faith without works is dead?" (James 2:17–20).

Jesus taught that "the kingdom of heaven is like unto a net, that was cast into the sea, and gathered of every kind: . . . when it was full, they drew to shore, . . . and gathered the good into vessels, but cast the bad away. So shall it be at the end of the world: the angels shall come forth, and sever the wicked from among the just, and shall cast them into the furnace of fire" (Matthew 13:47–50).

This is a rather strange parable. And yet it seems to describe things in the world as they really are. People of every kind come into the church, and the members gladly welcome them and strive to make their reception as smooth as possible. But there are habits to overcome, vices to jettison, and mindsets to be transformed by the power of the Holy Spirit. Gospel living becomes a narrowing process by which newly baptized saints proceed from the broad way to the strait and narrow way.

Priesthood leaders, teachers, and well-meaning friends offer counsel, and, most important, conscience begins to work its miracle in educating the initiate's desires. The person begins to sense that there are fewer things he or she can still do and get away with; the divine moral monitor that is given to everyone who comes into this life (John 1:9; D&C 84:46) directs toward the good, noble, and upright. Truly, "every thing which inviteth and enticeth to do good, and to love God, and to serve him, is inspired of God" (Moroni 7:13). Indeed, "strait is the gate, and narrow is the way, which leadeth unto life, and few there be that find it" (Matthew 7:14).

At first the new believer may feel that her new lifestyle is restrictive, perhaps even stifling. She may wonder whether she is losing control of her life. In a very real way, *she is,* for she is surrendering her will and moral agency to a higher power, to One who knows best. In speaking of a time in his own life when he chose to do things the Lord's way, President Boyd K. Packer said: "I determined that I would *give* Him the one thing that He would never take—my agency. I decided, by myself, that from that time on I would do things His way.

"That was a great trial for me, for I thought I was giving away the most precious thing I possessed. I was not wise enough in my youth to know that because I exercised my agency and decided myself, I was not *losing* it. It was *strengthened!*"[2]

The path to life—eternal life with God—is a narrow one. It is the path that leads to the tree of life, whose fruit brings peace, joy, love, light, fulfillment, and everlasting happiness. "Happiness is the object and design of our existence," the Prophet Joseph Smith declared, "and will be the end thereof, if we pursue the path that leads to it; and this path is virtue, uprightness, faithfulness, holiness, and keeping all the commandments of God."[3] King Benjamin, some five centuries after Lehi, invited us to "consider on the blessed and happy state of those that keep the commandments of God. For behold, they are blessed in all things, both temporal and spiritual; and if they hold out faithful to the end they are received into heaven, that thereby they may dwell with God in a state of never-ending happiness" (Mosiah 2:41).

ᴀ ɴᴅ ɪᴛ ᴄᴀᴍᴇ to pass that I did go forth and partake of the fruit thereof; and I beheld that it was most sweet, above all that I ever before tasted. Yea, and I beheld that the fruit thereof was white, to exceed all the whiteness that I had ever seen.

And as I partook of the fruit thereof it filled my soul with exceedingly great joy; wherefore, I began to be desirous that my family should partake of it also; for I knew that it was desirable above all other fruit.

1 Nephi 8:11–12

THE TREE OF life. The timeless token. The everlasting symbol. The perennial reminder that all we do in this life is but a prelude to all that shall come to pass in the life to come. The tree of life—a scriptural motif found in cultures throughout the world—reminds us that "this life is the time for men to prepare to meet God; yea, behold the day of this life is the day for men to perform their labors" (Alma 34:32).

In the Garden of Eden, the tree of life stood in contrast to the tree of knowledge of good and evil. The latter represented the path of mortality, the second estate, the period of probation, while the former pointed our first parents and us toward glorious resurrected immortality, the nature and kind of life enjoyed by those who have improved their time in mortality, have chosen to pursue righteousness, and have been true and faithful to their covenants. When Adam and Eve partook of the forbidden fruit and opened the way to mortality for all of us, God commanded that the tree of life be protected and shielded from our first parents, to ensure that they not partake of its fruit (Genesis 3:24; Moses 4:28–31). Is there not a type in this thing? Is

this not symbolic of God's order of things? Must not humankind first partake of mortality and then, after having been tried and tested in the furnace of affliction, after having demonstrated one's loyalty to the Lord, after having passed through death and undergone the refinement and expansion and liberation that come in the postmortal spirit world—is it not then the time for men and women to come forth from the grave in honor and power and glory in the resurrection of the just? Is it not at this time that we are permitted to partake of the fruit of the tree of life and go on to enjoy that abundant life, that eternal life with God of which the holy scriptures bear witness? Our Savior beckons to each one of us: "Come unto me and ye shall partake of the fruit of the tree of life; yea, ye shall eat and drink of the bread and the waters of life freely" (Alma 5:34).

Having planted the seed of faith within our souls—that is, having accepted Jesus Christ and his gospel as the only way to salvation (Alma 33:22–23; 34:4)—and having sought all our days to live that gospel and acquire and embody Christlike attributes, the tree of life begins to grow, as it were, within us. "And because of your diligence and your faith and your patience with the word in nourishing it, that it may take root in you, behold, by and by ye shall pluck the fruit thereof, which is most precious, which is sweet above all that is sweet, and which is white above all that is white, yea, and pure above all that is pure; and ye shall feast upon this fruit even until ye are filled, that ye hunger not, neither shall ye thirst" (Alma 32:42).

Happiness is not, however, a solitary condition. Christianity is a social endeavor. While salvation is an individual matter, exaltation in the highest heaven is a family affair. What person is there who finds sweet delight in things of the Spirit that does not yearn to share their spiritual riches, particularly with those closest to them? And so it is quite natural that Lehi, having partaken of the fruits of faithful discipleship and participated in the deepest joys of mortality, should want the same for his wife and children. Elder Neal A. Maxwell observed that "Parents who have, through gospel living, partaken of the fruit of the tree (which is the love of God) and who know the sweet sense of surrender in the kingdom of God will also be stirred, as Lehi was, for they too will be anxious, exceedingly anxious, that their families should partake also. Those who have known the sweetness of service in the kingdom and who have looked at life through the lens of the gospel will ever be restless with a divine discontent until their families do partake of that precious fruit and thereby witness for themselves."[4] It is in the home that we practice what is preached. The home becomes the great laboratory of life, the place where the fanciful facades are torn away and the masks of mortality come off. Indeed, "The home is so crucial that it is the source of our greatest failures as well as our greatest joys. It is one place that presses us to practice every major gospel principle, not just a few as may be the case in some fleeting and temporary relationships.

"Life in a family means we are known as we are, that our frailties are exposed and, hopefully, we then correct them."[5]

And as I cast my eyes round about, that perhaps I might discover my family also, I beheld a river of water; and it ran along, and it was near the tree of which I was partaking the fruit.

And I looked to behold from whence it came; and I saw the head thereof a little way off; and at the head thereof I beheld your mother Sariah, and Sam, and Nephi; and they stood as if they knew not whither they should go.

And it came to pass that I beckoned unto them; and I also did say unto them with a loud voice that they should come unto me, and partake of the fruit, which was desirable above all other fruit.

And it came to pass that they did come unto me and partake of the fruit also.

1 Nephi 8:13–16

LEHI MENTIONS, almost in passing, that he sees a river that runs beside the tree of life. Indeed, there were many things for Lehi to see within his dream, so many that he did not sense or realize what the river really represented. It was Nephi, who in vision beheld the very same things as his father (1 Nephi 11:3; 14:29), who looked more carefully and came away perhaps more sobered. Nephi pointed out that "the water which my father saw was filthiness; and so much was his mind swallowed up in other things that he beheld not the filthiness of the water. And I said unto [Laman and Lemuel] that it was an awful gulf, which separated the wicked from the tree of life, and also from the saints of God. And I said unto them that it was a representation of that awful hell, which the angel said unto me was prepared for the wicked" (1 Nephi 15:27–29). We might with value reflect on what things in our modern world keep us from the tree of life and from close association with those of the household of faith. What vanities and damnable distractions, if not repented of, will land our souls in hell when we pass

from this life and eventually secure to us a telestial tenement in eternity?

We might well adopt King Benjamin's attitude: "I cannot tell you all the things whereby ye may commit sin; for there are divers ways and means, even so many that I cannot number them. But this much I can tell you, that if ye do not watch yourselves, and your thoughts, and your words, and your deeds, and observe the commandments of God, and continue in the faith . . . , even unto the end of your lives, ye must perish. And now, O man [and woman], remember, and perish not" (Mosiah 4:29–30). The Savior delivered a similar warning in modern revelation when he cautioned us to "beware concerning yourselves" (D&C 84:43). President Joseph F. Smith once spoke of three great evils that threaten the Church and its members: the "flattery of prominent men in the world, false educational ideas, and sexual impurity."[6] President Ezra Taft Benson spoke of pride as the universal sin, the great vice, the great stumbling block to Zion,[7] while President Dieter F. Uchtdorf referred to pride as the "sin of self-elevation."[8] If you or I were to view a similar scene, what would we see in the filthy water? Would it be marital unfaithfulness? Gambling in all its ugly forms? Dishonesty at the workplace in the name of being a "smart businessman"? Pornographic magazines or internet sites? Family or child abuse, whether emotional, physical, or sexual? Cheating on exams or income taxes? The list could go on and on. We are certainly not at a loss, in this day of Satan's power, to identify some vice, some sin, that could possess our souls and destroy our lives.

How then do we avoid slipping off the gospel path into the waters of filthiness? How do we keep ourselves secure in the gospel harness until we are safely dead and freed from the lures of licentiousness? Alma taught a simple principle to his son Helaman that has profound implications. Alma counseled Helaman to keep the big picture, keep the distant scene in view. Note these words: "Preach unto them repentance, and

The tree of life was a common motif in many of William Morris's works.

faith on the Lord Jesus Christ; teach them to humble themselves and to be meek and lowly in heart; *teach them to withstand every temptation of the devil, with their faith on the Lord Jesus Christ*" (Alma 37:33; emphasis added). In short, Alma is teaching us all to "look to God and live" (Alma 37:47). Look to Christ! Look to the tree of life, to the gospel path, and stay on it. Like the apostle Peter, we must not allow our eyes to be deflected from our Master by the winds and the waves of sin and destruction (Matthew 14:22–33). We must trust Christ—that he can do for us all that he has promised. We must have confidence in Christ—confidence that the power of Christ is greater than any evil allurement. As Elder Jeffrey R. Holland has taught: "Most people in trouble end up crying, 'What was I thinking?' Well, whatever they were thinking, they weren't thinking of Christ. . . . So let us work a little harder at remembering Him."[9]

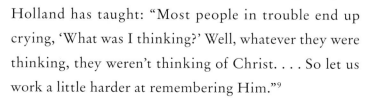

IT IS NOT ENOUGH for a parent to desire that their children and grandchildren partake of the fruit of the tree of life. Yearning is a very good start. Longing for their happiness is a noble beginning, but only a beginning. Praying for their success is fundamental, but the Father of us all certainly expects us as parents to be about the work of cultivating a climate of learning and spiritual growth and understanding. Hopes and dreams are translated into realities only when we rise from prayer and get to work. Lehi beckoned to Sariah and to his children to "come unto me, and partake of the fruit" (1 Nephi 8:15). And we must do likewise.

Nothing is more spiritually deadening and off-putting to members of a family, for example, than for Mom and Dad to act one way at home and another way entirely at church. When parents attempt to maintain a pious exterior in public—to play a kind, gentle, and loving role—while being dictatorial or autocratic at home, children begin to grow in cynicism, to conclude that the concept of "forever families" is a sham, and to perceive spirituality as merely an appearance to be maintained.

No one of us is a perfect parent, and no one of us conducts himself or herself in all family settings in just the right way; we slip, we stumble, and we fall, much more often than we would like. The beauty of parenting is that children can be remarkably forgiving, particularly when they sense that we are trying to be our best but fall short. But hypocrisy and self-righteousness are hard for a child to stomach. Pretending to be what we are not may have long-lasting results upon the souls of those who matter so very much to us. When parents "play church," as some young people describe it, children generally conclude that everyone else is doing the same and that "beauty all around" and "love at home" are nowhere to be found, which is simply not true.

Those whom we love will be enticed by righteousness to the extent that they sense it is an attractive quality. Similarly, children whose fathers and mothers lead and counsel in gentleness are far more likely to draw their children unto the Savior. Parents who have sought earnestly to be filled with the pure love of Christ; who are far more concerned with what their children are *becoming* than with what they are *doing;* whose own lives bespeak openness, breadth, a generosity of soul; and whose approach to commandment-keeping is more glad-hearted and spontaneous than rule-driven and pharisaic—these are the kinds of parents whose children feel drawn toward the light, and even if for a time they choose to leave the path, they will eventually return (Proverbs 22:6). The Savior uttered a profound truth when he said, "And *for their sakes* [the disciples] *I sanctify myself,* that they also might be sanctified through the truth" (John 17:19; emphasis added). Parents who sanctify themselves, who have made a choice in favor of gospel living, who strive to jettison from their lives any and all worldly distractions—such parents' words ring with authenticity and are far more likely to be felt in the hearts of loved ones.

While "come unto me" seems to be an invitation that only the sinless Son of Man could or should extend, there is a sense in which each of those who have partaken of the gospel banquet may rightfully invite others to "come unto me." It was not uncommon for the apostle Paul to encourage his new converts by inviting them to be as he was. Now to be sure, no one was more aware of his own foibles and weaknesses than Paul (see Romans 7). But Paul wasn't saying, "Come, live the flawless life just as I have." What he was saying was, "Come, partake of the bread of life and the living water, as I have. Come, involve yourselves in the body of believers, and receive nourishment and succor, as I have. Come unto Christ, forsake your sins, be transformed from the inside out, and become new creatures in Christ, as I have. Come, enjoy the blessing of loving your neighbor as yourselves, even as I have."

This invitation or teaching need not be either dramatic or sensational. Rather, the spontaneous testimony of a father bearing witness to his children in a family home evening of the sweet fruits of living the moral code of the Church works wonders. The gentle and sweet witness of a mother affirming the vital importance of celestial marriage while brushing her daughter's hair will reap eternal rewards. The spirit that comes into a family gathering as Grandpa speaks wistfully and inspirationally of memorable missionary experiences—these are the stuff out of which conversion and spiritual retention are made.

And it came to pass that I was desirous that Laman and Lemuel should come and partake of the fruit also; wherefore, I cast mine eyes towards the head of the river, that perhaps I might see them.

And it came to pass that I saw them, but they would not come unto me and partake of the fruit.

1 Nephi 8:17–18

LEHI HAS A BRIEF moment of rejoicing, for he sees in his dream/vision that his wife Sariah and his sons Sam and Nephi partake of the fruit of the tree of life (1 Nephi 8:16). Just as Mom and Dad feel the pains of little Becky's fall from her bicycle in their own bodies, and just as they mourn deeply with their teenage son Sterling when they learn that he has contracted a deadly disease, even so they are thrilled when one of their own makes a conscious choice to receive the gospel of Jesus Christ. Early in this dispensation, the Master revealed that "the worth of souls is great in the sight of God" (D&C 18:10). Why are souls worth so much to our Father and our Savior? Is it because each person is in reality a son or daughter of the Almighty? Is it because each boy and girl, every man and woman, has endless potential and unlimited possibilities? To be sure. But the revelation continues and shows, first and foremost, why souls are of inestimable worth: "For, behold, the Lord your Redeemer suffered death in the flesh; wherefore he suffered the pain of all men, that all men might repent and come unto him. And he hath risen again from the dead, that he might bring all men unto him, on conditions of repentance. And how great is his joy in the soul that repenteth!" (D&C 18:11–13).

The worth of souls is great because an infinite price has been paid for them. Truly, as the apostle Paul wrote, we are bought with a price; we are not our own (1 Corinthians 6:19–20; 7:23). Our Divine Redeemer suffered in both body and spirit in Gethsemane and on Golgotha. He felt the intense agony of our pains, our afflictions, our temptations, our sicknesses, our infirmities, our sins, and the bands of physical death (Alma 7:11–12). We have been redeemed by the precious blood of Christ (1 Peter 1:18–19). Jesus offered himself as an infinite and eternal sacrifice, and consequently, whatever he redeems is of infinite worth.

There is nothing more satisfying that witnessing your own child come alive to the things of the Spirit, develop an insatiable appetite for doctrinal truths, sing the hymns of Zion with vigor and enthusiasm, and pray with a yearning known only to those who have come to know the joy of their redemption. Like Ammon, parents' hearts are filled to overflowing; they are brim with joy (Alma 26). And yet, while the greatest joys in life are family joys, so also the greatest sorrows are family sorrows. No young parent supposes, in their wildest imagination, that the infant that is now bouncing on their lap will ever be, in later years, anything other than thoroughly committed to Christ and fully active and involved in the programs of the church. The Church of Jesus Christ is a family church, and "no other success can compensate for failure in the home."[10] The Church of Jesus Christ is in reality an auxiliary, and it exists to bless individuals and families, for the most important work we will ever do in the church will be done within the walls of our own homes.[11]

The Saints of God understand only too well that in the world to come it will be exalted families, not just glorified individuals, who will surround the heavenly throne and sing praises to the Lamb of God. Eternal life, which is the highest form of salvation, consists in (1) inheriting, receiving, and possessing the fulness of the glory and power of the Father, and (2) the continuation of the family unit into eternity (D&C 132:19). Elijah the prophet was sent to the Kirtland Temple on 3 April 1836 to confer the sealing power, the power to bind and unite families everlastingly. If he had not come, and if the keys of this sacred power had not been given to the Saints through the Prophet Joseph Smith, and if the people of earth are not able thereby to create an unbroken chain of souls back to Adam, the whole earth will "be utterly wasted at [Christ's] coming" (D&C 2:3). Why? Because the people of the earth will not have fulfilled their foreordained purpose—to establish a family order on earth patterned after the one in heaven. This is why a proper covenant marriage was so vital and important to the ancients. This is why it was so crucial that Abraham send his servant on a significant mission to identify a woman of covenant meet for his son Isaac (Genesis 24). Truly the family is the most important unit in time and in eternity.

AΠD I BEHELD a rod of iron, and it extended along the bank of the river, and led to the tree by which I stood.

And I also beheld a strait and narrow path, which came along by the rod of iron, even to the tree by which I stood; and it also led by the head of the fountain, unto a large and spacious field, as if it had been a world.

And I saw numberless concourses of people, many of whom were pressing forward, that they might obtain the path which led unto the tree by which I stood.

And it came to pass that they did come forth, and commence in the path which led to the tree.

1 Nephi 8:19–22

LEHI NOW beholds a rod of iron that extends along the bank of the river of filthy waters and that leads eventually to the tree of life (1 Nephi 8:19). The iron rod, "strong, and bright, and true,"[12] to which we hold in times of stress and distress and turmoil, keeps us rooted and grounded in faith and linked to our Lord. The Saints of the Most High are charged to "hold to the rod." And what is this anchor, this Godsend that enables us to pass safely through the tsunamis of the soul? Nephi explains simply that it is "the word of God" (1 Nephi 11:25), "and whoso would hearken unto the word of God, and would hold fast unto it, they would never perish; neither could the temptations and the fiery darts of the adversary overpower them unto blindness, to lead them away to destruction" (1 Nephi 15:24).

The scriptures are the word of God. When we read, study, and ponder over the meaning of holy writ, we are listening to words from an earlier time but words which have become, by the power of the Holy Spirit, eternally relevant. Because God's voice is Spirit and his Spirit is truth (D&C 88:66), when we hear the holy scriptures we are hearing the voice of the Almighty. This is exactly what the Lord revealed through Joseph Smith in June 1829 about the revelations he had received: "These words are not of men nor of man, but of me; wherefore, you shall testify they are of me and not of man; for it is my voice which speaketh them unto you; for they are given by my Spirit unto you, and by my power you can read them one to another; and save it were by my power you could not have them; wherefore, you can testify that you have heard my voice, and know my words" (D&C 18:34–36). When we hold to the scriptures, we align ourselves with the language, learning, and logic of scripture; we begin to think and reason like those holy men of God who spoke as they were moved upon by the Holy Ghost (2 Peter 1:21). When we hold to the scriptures as the word of God, we operate our lives by scriptural principles and thus render judgments that are wise and good.

The words of living prophets and apostles are the word of God. Through his covenant spokesmen, the Lord reveals his secrets (Amos 3:7), the mysteries of the kingdom—those things that can be known only by the power of the Spirit.[13] In a world blinded by sin, seers and revelators make known things which are not visible to the natural eye (Moses 6:36), matters that may be just around the corner and invisible to the masses. When we give heed to the words of his servants, we are promised that "the Lord God will disperse the powers of darkness from before you, and cause the heavens to shake for your good, and his name's glory" (D&C 21:6). That is, we will walk in the Son's light, and he will move heaven and earth to protect us. We hold to the rod—the words of living apostles and prophets—when we listen to, attend to, reflect on, and govern our behavior by them.

The voice of God's Holy Spirit is the word of God. We "hold to the rod" when we hold to his Spirit, and we chart a course that will keep us on the gospel path and cultivate the gift of the Holy Ghost in our lives. While eternal life is the greatest gift of God to us in eternity, the gift of the Holy Ghost is the greatest gift we can receive in this life.[14] If that is the case, then the followers of the Christ do all within their power to live worthy of that sacred guidance and influence; indeed, they strive never to do anything that would cost them the influence of the Holy Ghost. To hold to the Holy Spirit is to ask for it, nay, to plead for it in great earnestness, realizing that our ways are not God's ways and that our thoughts are not God's thoughts (Isaiah 55:8–9). To hold to the rod is do our best to think and feel and act as Jesus Christ, the Prototype of all saved beings,[15] thinks and feels and acts; it is to gain, as the apostle Paul encouraged, "the mind of Christ" (1 Corinthians 2:16).

All of these represent the word of God. And yet there is a grander way to view this matter: Christ himself is the Word of God. "In the beginning was the Word," John writes, "and the Word was with God, and the Word was God. The same was in the beginning with God" (John 1:1–2). Jesus is "the Word, even the messenger of salvation" (D&C 93:8). He is the Expression of the Father, the Answer to all the world's questions. To see him is to see the Father (John 14:9). When the risen Lord appeared to the Nephites, the people prayed to him directly, because he was with them (3 Nephi 19:22). "Seeing him, it was as though they saw the Father; praying to him, it was as though they prayed to the Father."[16] John the Revelator penned the following: "And I saw heaven opened, and behold a white horse; and he that sat upon him is called Faithful and True, and in righteousness he doth judge and make war; his eyes as a flame of fire; and he had on his head many crowns; and a name written, that no man knew, but himself. And he is clothed with a vesture dipped in blood; and his name is called The Word of God. And the armies which were in heaven followed him upon white horses, clothed in fine linen, white and clean. And out of his mouth proceedeth the word of God, and with it he will smite the nations; and he will rule them with the word of his mouth; and he treadeth the winepress in the fierceness and wrath of Almighty God. And he hath on a vesture, and on his thigh a name written, KING OF KINGS, AND LORD OF LORDS" (JST, Revelation 19:11–16).

We "hold to the rod," to Jesus Christ, when we accept him as Lord and Savior and open ourselves to the transforming power of his atonement. To choose Christ is to choose to be changed. We hold to him when we covenant never to forsake him, his kingdom, or his anointed servants. We hold to the rod of Jesus when we speak his name with reverence and reflect on his substitutionary offering with awe and gratitude. To choose Christ is to remain steadfast in the faith, to be constant, consistent, and immovable until we breathe our last and pass through that veil that separates time from eternity.

Nephi also beheld a narrow path that led from the large and spacious field to the tree of life (1 Nephi 8:20). This is the gospel path, the course we take when we exercise faith in the Lord Jesus Christ, repent of our sins, are baptized by immersion for the remission of sins, receive the gift of the Holy Ghost by the laying on of hands, and endure faithfully to the end of our mortal lives. Broad is the gate that leads to death, while strait (narrow) is the gate that leads to life (Matthew 7:13–14; D&C 132:22–25). Toward the end of his second book, Nephi will inquire: "And now, my beloved brethren, after ye have gotten into this strait and narrow path, I would ask if all is done? Behold, I say unto you, Nay; for ye have not come thus far save it were by the word of Christ with unshaken faith in him, relying wholly upon the merits of him who is mighty to save. Wherefore, ye must press forward with a steadfastness in Christ, having a perfect brightness of hope, and a love of God and of all men. Wherefore, if ye shall press forward, feasting upon the word of Christ, and endure to the end, behold, thus saith the Father: Ye shall have eternal life" (2 Nephi 31:19–20).

Almost everyone wants to be happy, wants to find joy and fulfillment in living. Lehi sees that large numbers of people seek to find the one way, the only way, the gospel way (1 Nephi 8:21); at least they have an initial desire to get on the path that leads to the tree of life. Unfortunately, not all of these hold to the rod, stay the course, and arrive at their destination. Some enter the way of salvation and move forward, only to be confronted by a "mist of darkness" that causes them to lose their way. A second group gets onto the path, navigates the course all the way to the tree, and then partakes of the fruit. Sadly,

Tree of life stone carving from a mosque at Ahmedabad, Gujarat, India.

they shrink in embarrassment beneath the mocking crowds that beckon from the great and spacious building (1 Nephi 8:24–28). Lehi then beholds a third group, "multitudes pressing forward" who catch hold of the rod, hold tightly to the standard, stay in the mainstream of gospel living, and eventually fall down at the tree, partake of the fruit, and, we would presume, remain true and faithful thereafter (1 Nephi 8:30). *Multitudes.*

What a comfort to those who wonder sometimes if anyone will make it! And then, of course, there are those whose ears are attuned to an entirely different voice, those who have no intention whatsoever of submitting to a higher will or surrendering to a nobler cause, those who spurn the way of holiness (Isaiah 35:8) and feel their way blindly toward the great and spacious building (1 Nephi 8:31–32). This is the story of life, Lehi's Parable of the Path.

MANY A PERSON hears the message of salvation, is impressed with its reasonableness, is touched by the power of the Spirit regarding its truthfulness, and receives baptism into the Lord's Church at the hands of authorized servants; he or she has entered into that path which leads to life eternal. At the close of his second book, Nephi inquires: "And now . . . , after ye have gotten into this strait and narrow path, I would ask if all is done? Behold, I say unto you, Nay; for ye have not come thus far save it were by the word of Christ with unshaken faith in him, relying wholly upon the merits of him who is mighty to save" (2 Nephi 31:19). That is, once you have become a member of the Church of Jesus Christ, have accepted the tenets of the faith, have repented and been washed clean of your sins, have you arrived? Have you, at this point in your journey, received fully the gift of eternal life? To this point, God has carried out *his* part of the gospel covenant: he has delivered the word of truth, made available the Atoning One as a ransom for your sins, and has supplied his righteousness in exchange for your sinfulness. God the Father has made, in the words of the

apostle Paul, Christ the Son, the only one "who knew no sin," to be "sin for us" so that "we might be made the righteousness of God in him" (2 Corinthians 5:21). O the mystery of God's Great Exchange. Since fallen man cannot merit anything of himself (Alma 22:14), those who exercise faith in the Redeemer enough to be baptized become recipients of "the merits, and mercy, and grace of the Holy Messiah" (2 Nephi 2:8). Christ pleads our cause on the basis of his righteous works and his redeeming blood (D&C 45:3–5).

Then do men and women have no responsibility for their salvation after baptism? Is it truly the case, as some in the Christian world assert, that once we have accepted Jesus as Savior, our salvation is secure and nothing we do thereafter will have any effect on our eternal destiny? Both reason and scripture proclaim with a voice of thunder: Those who have gotten onto the strait and narrow path are expected to manifest their faith through their faithfulness. Those who have received Jesus as Savior are obligated to surrender to him as the Lord of their lives. Those who claim to be disciples must strive to discipline their lives—must deny themselves all ungodliness, take up their cross daily, and follow Him (Luke 9:23; Moroni 10:32). In short, those who claim to love the Lord are to keep his commandments (John 14:15).

In that light, Nephi speaks of the Christian's part of the gospel covenant: "Wherefore, if ye shall press forward, feasting upon the word of Christ, and endure to the end, behold, thus saith the Father: Ye shall have eternal life" (2 Nephi 31:20). This is the fifth principle of the gospel—enduring to the end. To press forward with a steadfastness in Christ is to move ahead with consistency, constancy, and certitude. It is to be available, dependable, and flexible. True disciples learn to roll with the punches, to be patient with delays, to persevere through distractions, to refuse to be knocked off course by criticism. To be steadfast is not necessarily to be sinless, but rather to be determined, fixed, focused on the goal of exaltation, dedicated to fighting the good fight, finishing the course, and keeping the faith (2 Timothy 4:7).

D&C 117:13 is fascinating: "And *when he* [Oliver Granger, the agent of the First Presidency] *falls he shall rise again, for his sacrifice shall be more sacred unto me than his increase,* saith the Lord" (emphasis added). This

passage fills my soul with hope, optimism, and excitement that the righteous and holy Being we worship will work with, be patient with, and offer us an opportunity to get up and dust ourselves off whenever we fall. Character is not a product of a sinless life, not a result of never making an error of judgment, but rather never staying down once we have fallen. We show what we're made of and our determination to follow Christ by getting up and dusting ourselves off at least one more time than we fall. In so doing, we demonstrate our acceptance of the divine offer to us to re-group, re-work, and re-commit ourselves to the Christian life.

In the language of the risen Lord, "whoso repenteth and is baptized in my name shall be filled; and if he endureth to the end, behold, *him will I hold guiltless* before my Father at that day when I shall stand to judge the world" (3 Nephi 27:16; emphasis added). It is not the case that such a one has lived a flawless life, has been free of sin or void of guilt. Rather, the Lord honors and esteems such a person for staying true to their covenants until they have passed through the veil of death; the Lord *holds* or *accounts* or *treats* such a man or woman as though they are guiltless, for they have proven loyal to the One who *did* keep the law of God perfectly. They have thereby looked to and leaned heavily upon "the merits, and mercy, and grace of the Holy Messiah" (2 Nephi 2:8).

Those who have true faith in Jesus Christ—who have total *trust* in his power, complete *confidence* in his ability to sanctify and save, and a ready *reliance* upon his enabling power—will always have hope in Christ (Moroni 7:40–42). Hope is assurance, anticipation, expectation. Elder Russell M. Nelson has taught that "*faith* is rooted in Jesus Christ. *Hope* centers in his Atonement. *Charity* is manifest in the 'pure love of Christ' (see Moroni 7:47). These three attributes [intertwine] and may not always be precisely distinguished. Together they become our tether to the celestial kingdom."[17] To have faith in Christ is to know, by the power of the Holy Ghost, what he can do for humanity; to have hope in Christ is to know, by that same power, *what he will do for me.* It is a personal assurance. But why does loving God and our fellowman follow that faith and hope? Simply this: one who has enjoyed the blessings of the Atonement and has had sin and guilt remitted is a recipient of charity, the pure love of Christ.

Elder Jeffrey R. Holland has written: "The greater definition of 'the pure love of Christ,' . . . is not what we as Christians try but largely fail to demonstrate toward others but rather what Christ totally succeeded in demonstrating toward us. *True* charity has been known only once. It is shown perfectly and purely in Christ's unfailing, ultimate, and atoning love for us. It is Christ's love for us that 'suffereth long, and is kind, and envieth not.' It is his love for us that is not 'puffed up . . . , not easily provoked, thinketh no evil,' . . . that 'beareth all things, believeth all things, hopeth all things, endureth all things.' It is as demonstrated in Christ that 'charity never faileth.' It is that charity—his pure love for us—without which we would be nothing, hopeless, of all men and women most miserable. Truly, those found possessed of the blessings of his love at the last day—the Atonement, the Resurrection, eternal life, eternal promise—surely it shall be well with them."[18] President Dieter F. Uchtdorf has taught: "Hope is one leg of a three-legged stool, together with faith and charity. These three

stabilize our lives regardless of the rough or uneven surfaces we might encounter at the time."[19]

Men and women who partake of the fruit of our Lord's suffering begin to "sing the song of redeeming love" (Alma 5:26). They come to feel a deep sense of gratitude and love for him who loved us first (1 John 4:19). That love then expands from Him who begat us to include those who are begotten by him (1 John 5:1). Indeed, "we know that we have passed from death unto life, because we love the brethren" (1 John 3:14). And so pressing forward, loving God and God's children, linked with regular and consistent feasting on the word of God, allow one to partake of salvation or eternal life, the greatest of all the gifts of God (D&C 6:13; 14:7). Saints of the Most High who are so equipped, so empowered, so riveted on righteousness, may press their way through the mists of darkness, the "temptations of the devil," which otherwise would "[blind] the eyes, and [harden] the hearts of the children of men, and [lead] them away into broad roads, that they perish and are lost" (1 Nephi 12:17; compare 1 Nephi 15:24).

And After they had partaken of the fruit of the tree they did cast their eyes about as if they were ashamed.

1 Nephi 8:25

WHAT LEADS the people of God to become ashamed? To be ashamed is to be disconcerted, to be flustered, literally, "out of concert." To be disconcerted is to be disturbed because something has upset one's progress, spoiled the plans, or defeated the expectations.[20] In short, it is to be distressed because things didn't turn out the way we had expected. Sometimes people who have come out of the world into the gospel of Jesus Christ suppose that after their baptism everything will continue as before, that life will go on as usual. They soon discover that conversion to the way of the Master is not only a change of pace; it is a revolution, a revolt against many old ways and a growing revulsion for the telestial trappings all about us. To some extent, as the Holy Ghost begins to work upon our hearts and to adjust our vision, we come to hate many things we before loved and to love a surprising number of things we once hated. Conversion entails a mighty change of heart, not just a slight alteration in how one spends the Sabbath. It may entail a major change in friendships, in places we frequent, in entertainment we consume, or in words we do not speak.

One simply cannot hold to the past—meaning our fallen way of life—and expect to delight in the ways of goodness and decency. If a person who has come into the Lord's church finds himself pining for the "good ole days" of the past, languishing and lingering and looking back like Lot's wife (Genesis 19:26), he has not undergone a true conversion to the faith. If a person discovers herself uncomfortable talking of religious things and thinking about spiritual matters Monday through Saturday, as well as on Sunday, she has not entered into the faith sufficiently to withstand temptation and trials. She has not been converted. "One is converted when he sees with his eyes what he ought to see; when he hears with his ears what he ought to hear; and when he understands with his heart what he ought to understand. And what he ought to see, hear, and understand is truth—eternal truth—and then practice it. That is conversion."[21]

Why would one partake of the fruit of the tree of life and feel embarrassed by so doing? Could it be that the putative Christian, the reputed disciple, has not made an unconditional surrender to the Lord and his kingdom? Might it be the case that the person finds the lure of worldliness to be more powerful than the Spirit's quiet and sensitive enticement to do good? Jesus Christ offers deliverance from the superficial and the shallow. He offers a saving alternative to programs that are woefully deficient or even plainly perverse. His way, the gospel way, is easy to those who pursue it with single-mindedness. It is more difficult for those who embark on the Christian cause with hesitation or reservation. Those who have charted their course and pointed themselves toward the abundant life in Christ have their challenges, their difficulties, like

Persian rug displaying the tree of life.

anyone else. They meet such roadblocks, however, with courage and perspective, with a quiet confidence born of the Spirit. These individuals have no difficulty living the gospel. It is not hard. It is not burdensome. For followers of the lowly Nazarene, living the gospel is a lifting and liberating experience. In the ultimate

sense, President Brigham Young explained, "the man or woman who enjoys the spirit of our religion has no trials; but the man or woman who tries to live according to the Gospel of the Son of God, and at the same time clings to the spirit of the world, has trials and sorrows acute and keen, and that, too, continually.

"This is the deciding point, the dividing line. They who love and serve God with all their hearts rejoice evermore, pray without ceasing, and in everything give thanks; but they who try to serve God and still cling to the spirit of the world, have got on two yokes—the yoke of Jesus and the yoke of the devil, and they will have plenty to do. They will have a warfare inside and outside, and the labor will be very galling, for they are directly in opposition one to the other. Cast off the yoke of the enemy, and put on the yoke of Christ, and you will say that his yoke is easy and his burden is light."[22]

And I also cast my eyes round about, and beheld, on the other side of the river of water, a great and spacious building; and it stood as it were in the air, high above the earth.

1 Nephi 8:26

THE GREAT and spacious building, which Nephi explains represents the pride and wisdom of the world (1 Nephi 11:35), may not be as much a place as a spiritual condition, a state of mind. It may be an attractive domicile, a spectacular site for gathering those who wander blindly in search of telestial titillation. But it really has precious little to offer, for it is a building without foundation, or, more correctly, a church whose founder is the devil (1 Nephi 14:17), and it will eventually crumble and fall to the dust (1 Nephi 14:17; 22:23).

Double-minded men and women are unstable in all their ways (James 1:8). That instability manifests itself dramatically in their inability to choose between Zion and Babylon. Zion has much to offer, the unstable assert, especially on Sundays, and it's always heartwarming to sing and pray and teach and learn and bear testimony once a week. Why, it's a highlight of the week, a kind of icing on the cake. Besides, everyone needs a little religion, don't they? But balance is what we need; variety is the spice of life, they say. Surely well-adjusted persons who have their feet on the ground

and are thereby in touch with the "real world" out there feel some need to be "balanced." C. S. Lewis has wisely observed that too often men and women have "substituted *religion* for God—as if navigation were substituted for arrival, or battle for victory, or wooing for marriage, or in general the means for the end." Further, "there is danger in the very concept of *religion*. It carries the suggestion that this is one more department of life, an extra department added to the economic, the social, the intellectual, the recreational, and all the rest. But that whose claims are infinite can have no standing as a department. Either it is an illusion or else our whole life falls under it. We have no non-religious activities, only religious and irreligious."[23]

In a revelation given to Joseph Smith on 7 August 1831, the Lord of the Sabbath counseled: "And that thou mayest more fully keep thyself unspotted from the world, thou shalt go to the house of prayer and offer up thy sacraments upon my holy day; for verily this is a day appointed unto you to rest from your labors, and to pay thy devotions unto the Most High." Now notice the following penetrating directive: "Nevertheless *thy vows shall be offered up in righteousness on all days and at all times*" (D&C 59:9–11; emphasis added). Simply stated, the gospel of Jesus Christ is a consuming endeavor, an all-encompassing enterprise, a 24/7 life.

True disciples do not expect to proffer a tithe of their lives to the Almighty and then to receive hereafter all that the Father has. Citizens of Zion, those who have come out of the world and counted the cost of following Christ, would never trifle with the spirit of grace and godliness by surrendering only a portion of the self. Again from C. S. Lewis, who offered such penetrating insight into the human soul: "Christ says 'Give me All. I don't want so much of your time and so much of your money and so much of your work: I want You. I have not come to torment your natural self, but to kill it. No half-measures are any good. I don't want to cut off a branch here and a branch there, I want to have the whole tree down. I don't want to drill the tooth, or crown it, or stop it, but to have it out. Hand over the whole natural self, all the desires which you think innocent as well as the ones you think wicked—the whole

outfit. I will give you a new self instead. In fact, I will give you Myself: my own will shall become yours.'"[24]

Those who feel ashamed after taking the fruit of the tree of life have spent far too much time and energy being obsessed with the "vain imaginations," the empty and superficial promises and professions of the worldly wise (1 Nephi 12:18). On the other hand, persons who have cast their lot with the Lord Jesus Christ and his gospel, who have counted the cost and measured the manner of devotion required to maintain Christian discipleship (Luke 14:28), and who have proclaimed that in their lives it will be "the Kingdom of God or nothing"—these are they who will have the moral courage, like Nephi, to give no heed to the temptings and tauntings of those who proselyte from the great and spacious building (1 Nephi 8:33).

AПD IT was filled with people, both old and young, both male and female; and their manner of dress was exceedingly fine; and they were in the attitude of mocking and pointing their fingers towards those who had come at and were partaking of the fruit.

And after they had tasted of the fruit they were ashamed, because of those that were scoffing at them; and they fell away into forbidden paths and were lost.

1 Nephi 8:27–28

THE GATHERING place for the worldly wise is described as "great" (large) and "spacious." No doubt one must pass through the *wide* gate in order to get on the *broad* road that leads to it, the road *most* taken. This hellish hangout is open to all shapes and sizes and ages of boys and girls and men and women, for hubris knows no boundaries or class distinctions, and high-mindedness has no age restrictions. One thing all the residents have in common, however, is their obsession with the best and the finest, the flashiest and the most expensive. And why are they mocking and ridiculing those who have gone through the *narrow* gate onto the *strait* path that leads to the tree of life? So very often, people mock what they cannot understand. They think it foolish to devote oneself to a noble cause, ridiculous to be committed and converted to things which may not be seen or felt or experienced by the natural senses. They know only the physical and the fanciful. Having glutted themselves on natural phenomena, they are unable to perceive those insights and joys that come from the supernatural world. Unsatisfied with what they have, they wander aimlessly and endlessly in search of some new stimulation, some novel sensation. Their threshold for thrills is forever rising, and so it becomes more and more difficult to find pleasure and satisfaction. They laugh to mask their fear and their frustration. They point the finger of scorn at the righteous to reassure themselves that their way is indeed better.

If one looks carefully, he or she can read the signs of wear and tear in the faces of those who have chosen to love and give devoted service to either questionable or diabolical causes. Error and wickedness take their terrible tolls upon the hearts and countenances of those who choose divergent paths; the wheels of waywardness grind away slowly but inexorably to produce a type of demented character that will never know peace of mind. Both Zion and Babylon make definite demands of its citizens, and as the millennial day approaches each of these communities will insist upon the total devotion and complete consecration of its municipals. Thus fewer and fewer persons will remain lukewarm. The myopic and misguided of the world will grow in cynicism and confusion; the ungodly will, as time goes by, sink ever deeper into a despair known only to those engulfed in iniquity. Wickedness will widen and malevolence will multiply until the citizens of Babylon seal themselves to him who is the father of all lies, the father of damnation. Money is not the answer. Neither wealth nor social esteem is the answer. "Why should we labor this unpleasant point?" Hugh Nibley asked. "Because the Book of Mormon labors it, for our special benefit. Wealth is a jealous master who will not be served half-heartedly and will suffer no rival—not even God. . . . In return for unquestioning obedience, wealth promises security, power, position, and honors, in fact anything in this world. . . . The more important wealth is, the less important it is how one gets it."[25] On the other hand, "Zion must arise and put on her beautiful garments" (D&C 82:14). The Church of the Lamb will continue to require the tithes and offerings and donations and energies of its members until that day when a full and consecrated life is realized and achieved. The Saints of the Most High will thus establish a heaven on earth and eventually receive the glorious assurance of exaltation in the highest heaven.

Jesus uttered a profound truth when he said: "I receive not honour from men" (John 5:41; compare 8:54). While Jesus loved those among whom he walked and talked and ministered; while he sought diligently to turn the hearts of sinners to him and to his gospel; and while he certainly longed to have all men look to him for redemption and salvation, he did not court favor; he was no respecter of persons. He did not put on airs, nor was he in any way motivated or impressed by this world's pecking order. Jesus looked to his Father for approval. While he certainly wanted all men to love him and follow him, he would not resort to cheap tactics or sensational displays to gain disciples (Matthew 4:5–7). His feelings of worth did not derive from the petty plaudits of mortal men and women. Nor should ours.

We have been counseled by the Master not to fast, or pray, or serve the poor to be seen of men. Those who do so, who manage appearances in order to heap applause upon their deeds, "have their reward" (Matthew 6:2, 5, 16; 3 Nephi 13:2, 5, 16). Those who look to the masses rather than to their hearts or the counsel of the Lord's servants in deciding what is right and what is wrong will be forever in flux; social consensus shifts over time and is a moving target. Those who operate their lives in order to please the public will find their fans to be fickle and their fame fleeting. The people of the covenant cannot afford to yield themselves to such superficiality. The call to discipleship is a call to a higher righteousness. The Saints are asked to put off the natural man, put away the toys of this telestial world, and grow up in the Lord. They are summoned to be obedient, to keep the commandments, to manifest "by a godly walk and conversation, that they are worthy" of membership in the church and kingdom of God (D&C 20:69). They covenant to take upon them the sacred name of Jesus Christ, to bear the same with fidelity and devotion, and to behave as Christians. In short, they covenant before God and man to see to it that their actions evidence their Christian commitment. Disciples are expected to have clean hands. But there is more. Life in Christ is more than correct behavior, more than appropriate actions, more than what we *do*. It is being. It is what we *are*. True disciples seek that sanctifying influence that derives from the Holy Spirit,

so that gradually they begin to do the right things for the right reasons. Life in Christ is characterized by pure attitudes, motives, and desires. Disciples are expected to have pure hearts (see Matthew 6:1–8, 16–18; 3 Nephi 13:1–8, 16–18).

We might suppose that service of any kind has merit. There is, however, a spiritual motivation that impels us to righteous deeds, that sanctifies giver and receiver. When the doers of the deed are single in their intent; when the givers focus far more on the one to be assisted than on their own comfort or appearance; when the alms, the offering is made wholly for the blessing and good of the receiver, then lasting good is accomplished and those involved know that the Lord is pleased. What then is the duty of the developing disciple? What does a man or a woman do whose motives are not absolutely pure? In short, what about many of us who hold membership in the Church of Jesus Christ? Do we sit back and avoid deeds of service because our desires are not yet sanctified? Do we refrain from visiting teaching or home teaching, for example, because our motivation is presently clouded by the spirit of inspection rather than of stewardship and covenant? Certainly not. We have a labor to perform, a work to do in order to bear off the kingdom of God triumphant. And Zion—as well as its municipals, its citizenry—is being established "in process of time" (Moses 7:21). Simply stated, disciples of Christ do not wait to be transformed before they proceed in the work of the ministry. Missionaries do not wait in their apartments for an unusual outpouring of the Spirit before they approach the first door. Rather, they seek to purify themselves from sin, pray intently for divine direction and power, and then proceed, confident that the needed endowment will be forthcoming when the Lord sees fit to send it. The quest for a pure heart is the quest for pure motives and desires. Surely one of the most significant requests disciples make of their Master is for the cleansing and purification of their motives, a greater desire to do the right things for the right reason. To have a situation wherein the left hand does not know what the right hand is doing (Matthew 6:3; 3 Nephi 13:3) is to be in a condition where there is no ulterior motivation, no hidden agenda, no selfish

purposes for our actions. In one sense, then, the great challenge of true disciples is to rise above self—self-regard, self-inspection, self-promotion.

The Saints of God are in fact "a chosen generation, a royal priesthood, an holy nation, a peculiar people." The Mediator of the covenant has called them "out of darkness into his marvellous light" (1 Peter 2:9). They are *peculiar*—different from the norm, set apart from the average, driven and impelled by a higher standard. They are *peculiar*—purchased, ransomed by their Redeemer; they are not their own, they have been bought with a price, the price of the precious blood of Christ, and they know it (1 Corinthians 7:22–23). Solid in their faith, they are secure in their commitment to the gospel of Jesus Christ. Drenched in sweet certitude, they move along on the gospel path and are kept from daily distractions by their faith on the Lord Jesus Christ (Alma 37:33).

And now I, Nephi, do not speak all the words of my father.

But, to be short in writing, behold, he saw other multitudes pressing forward; and they came and caught hold of the end of the rod of iron; and they did press their way forward, continually holding fast to the rod of iron, until they came forth and fell down and partook of the fruit of the tree.

And he also saw other multitudes feeling their way towards that great and spacious building.

And it came to pass that many were drowned in the depths of the fountain; and many were lost from his view, wandering in strange roads.

1 Nephi 8:29–32

WE MUST remind ourselves, while reading the first nine chapters in the Book of Mormon, that Nephi is abridging the record of his father Lehi (1 Nephi 1:17). While we presume that Nephi received the same vision as his father (1 Nephi 14:29), Nephi did not include everything that Lehi said or did. As touched upon earlier, the third group of people in the Parable of the Paths press forward and take hold of the iron rod. How many did so? *Multitudes!*

In comparison to the number of wicked souls at any given time, perhaps the number of faithful followers seems small. But what of the children who have died before the age of accountability—billions of little ones from the days of Adam to the time of the Second Coming, whom the scriptures affirm are saved in the celestial kingdom (D&C 137:10)? What of those through the ages who never had the opportunity to hear the message of salvation in mortal life but who (because of their yearnings for light and truth) will receive it in the postmortal world? And, we might ask, what of the hosts who qualified for salvation from Enoch's city,

Melchizedek's Salem, the golden era of the Nephites, or other societies of which we have no record? (see D&C 49:8). What of the countless billions of children who will be born during the glorious millennial era—during a time when disease, death, and sin have neither sting nor victory over humankind? This will be that time of which the revelations speak, when "children shall grow up without sin unto salvation" (D&C 45:58). Given the renewed and paradisiacal state of the earth, it may well be that more persons will live on the earth during the thousand years of our Lord's reign—persons who are of at least a terrestrial nature—than the combined total of all who have lived during the previous six thousand years of the earth's temporal existence. Indeed, who can count the number of saved beings in eternity? Our God, who is triumphant in all battles against the forces of evil, will surely be victorious in the numbers of his children who will be saved.

Elder Bruce R. McConkie taught: "As members of the Church, if we chart a course leading to eternal life; if we begin the processes of spiritual rebirth, and are going in the right direction; if we chart a course of sanctifying our souls, and degree by degree are going in that direction; and if we chart a course of becoming perfect, and, step by step and phase by phase, are perfecting our souls by overcoming the world, then it is absolutely guaranteed—there is no question whatever about it—we shall gain eternal life. Even though we have spiritual rebirth ahead of us, perfection ahead of us, the full degree of sanctification ahead of us, if we chart a course and follow it to the best of our ability in this life, then when we go out of this life we'll continue in exactly that same course. We'll no longer be subject to the passions and appetites of the flesh. We will have passed successfully the tests of this mortal probation and in due course we'll get the fulness of our Father's kingdom—and that means eternal life in his everlasting presence."[26]

We must never forget that there is no ceiling on the number of saved beings in eternity, no cap, no quota by which our Father must and will be governed. President Joseph F. Smith, who beheld in vision the postmortal spirit world only six weeks before his own death and entrance therein, remarked: "As I pondered over these

things which are written"—1 Peter 3 and 4—"the eyes of my understanding were opened, and the Spirit of the Lord rested upon me, and I saw the hosts of the dead, both small and great. And there were gathered together in one place"—we know it as Paradise—"*an innumerable company of the spirits of the just, who had been faithful in the testimony of Jesus while they lived in mortality. . . .* All these had departed the mortal life, firm in the hope of a glorious resurrection, through the grace of God the Father and his Only Begotten Son, Jesus Christ" (D&C 138:11–14; emphasis added).

We do not suppose that the gospel journey of those who proved faithful is any different than others, that their quest is any easier, or their challenges are any less. Entrance into God's church does not keep travelers from slipping occasionally into potholes. The natural storms of life come to those who have chosen the right just as they do to those who have either made no choice or those who have knowingly decided to defect. In the words of the Savior, God "maketh his sun to rise on the evil and on the good, and sendeth rain on the just and on the unjust" (Matthew 5:45; see also 3 Nephi

12:45). The Prophet Joseph Smith explained that "it is a false idea that the Saints will escape all the judgments, whilst the wicked suffer; for all flesh is subject to suffer, and 'the righteous shall hardly escape;' still many of the Saints will escape, for the just shall live by faith; yet many of the righteous shall fall a prey to disease, to pestilence, etc., by reason of the weakness of the flesh, and yet be saved in the Kingdom of God. So that it is an unhallowed principle to say that such and such have transgressed because they have been preyed upon by disease or death, for all flesh is subject to death; and the Savior has said, 'Judge not, lest ye be judged.'"[27]

Those who make their way down the narrowing path, the "way of holiness" (Isaiah 35:8), press forward through insults, move ahead through challenging questions, stay on course in spite of constant invitations to deviate or be distracted. It is worth noting what the revelations of God say about those who inherit the celestial kingdom: These are they "who overcome by faith" (D&C 76:53). They do not make it to the tree of life from sheer grit. While a certain measure of discipline is always required in facing life's foes head-on, as Paul taught, the just have come to live *by faith* (Romans 1:17; emphasis added). They do not rely upon their own strength or upon the arm of flesh, for they have learned, as Ammon proclaimed, "I know that I am nothing; as to my strength I am weak; therefore I will not boast of myself, but I will boast of my God, for in his strength I can do all things" (Alma 26:12; compare Philippians 4:13). Power to overcome does not come through programs, no matter how inspired. Rather, power is in the Person of Jesus Christ. Men and women of faith have come to rely *wholly* and *only* on their Lord and Master, for he is mighty to save (2 Nephi 31:19; Moroni 6:4).

"Continually holding fast to the rod of iron" (1 Nephi 8:30) entails turning daily to the holy scriptures for comfort and guidance; listening to, studying, and heeding our Church leaders' messages; cultivating the spirit of revelation in our lives; and yielding our hearts unto the Savior, striving to do things in his way. *Continually* implies without interruption. True Saints do not take vacations from the gospel, from church attendance, or from meaningful service. We are in this for the long haul, and to endure to the end is to be "steadfast and immovable, always abounding in good works, that Christ, the Lord God Omnipotent, may seal you his, that you may be brought to heaven, that ye may have everlasting salvation and eternal life" (Mosiah 5:15). Again, this is not about discipline alone; it is about a *disposition.* To choose Christ is to choose to be changed. It is to seek a change that is not just a cosmetic alteration but a transformation from the inside out. The Holy Ghost is a sanctifier, and one of his major tasks is to change our nature from carnal to righteous; from lust to genuine love; from greed to self-lessness; from critical to complimentary; from solitary to gregarious; from petty to magnanimous—in short, from death to life. Such conversion comes by virtue of the atoning blood of Christ, and the medium for that conversion is the Spirit.

Many of the world's population have no interest in spiritual things and no desire whatsoever to know or to please God. To speak to them of faith or revelation or atonement or salvation is to speak words devoid of meaning. Why? Because the natural man—the unre-deemed man or woman, the person who has received

neither the revealed witness of the Spirit nor its purging and sanctifying powers in his or her life—cannot discern spiritual things and considers them to be foolish (1 Corinthians 2:11–14). Such a one hasn't the slightest inclination or interest in the strait and narrow path, much less the tree of life at its end. Such a one takes the most direct path to spiritual destruction, heading directly to the great and spacious building. Blinded by their own waywardness, "walking in darkness at noonday" (D&C 95:6), this group feels their way toward the domicile of demons. And of course, once their dues are paid and their place secured, they shout scorn and revel in ridicule. They proselyte others to share in their bitterness. Truly, as the angel declared to King Benjamin, natural men are enemies to God (Mosiah 3:19), indeed, enemies to their own souls, enemies to their own happiness and well-being (see Alma 41:10–11).

OR IT CAME to pass after I had desired to know the things that my father had seen, and believing that the Lord was able to make them known unto me, as I sat pondering in mine heart I was caught away in the Spirit of the Lord, yea, into an exceedingly high mountain, which I never had before seen, and upon which I never had before set my foot.

And the Spirit said unto me: Behold, what desirest thou?

And I said: I desire to behold the things which my father saw.

And the Spirit said unto me: Believest thou that thy father saw the tree of which he hath spoken?

And I said: Yea, thou knowest that I believe all the words of my father.

And when I had spoken these words, the Spirit cried with a loud voice, saying: Hosanna to the Lord, the most high God; for he is God over all the earth, yea, even above all. And blessed art thou, Nephi, because thou believest in the Son of the most high God; wherefore, thou shalt behold the things which thou hast desired.

And behold this thing shall be given unto thee for a sign, that after thou hast beheld the tree which bore the fruit which thy father tasted, thou shalt also behold a man descending out of heaven, and him shall ye witness; and after ye have witnessed him ye shall bear record that it is the Son of God.

1 Nephi 11:1–7

SINCE THE TIME the Book of Mormon rolled off the Grandin Press in March 1830, Nephi has been heralded for his tenacious obedience, as well as his Christian courage. He embodies such virtues and gifts as gratitude (he was "born of goodly parents"; 1 Nephi 1:1), humility ("I do not know the meaning of all things"; 1 Nephi 11:17), faith ("I will go and do . . . for I know"; 1 Nephi 3:7), spirituality ("I was led by the Spirit, not knowing"; 1 Nephi 4:6), and magnanimity ("I did frankly forgive them"; 1 Nephi 7:21). Nephi showed tremendous respect for his father Lehi and always deferred to him on matters of leadership and stewardship. At the same time, Nephi's spiritual sensitivity and maturity were such that he comprehended a significant principle—that God will manifest himself to all who seek Him in diligence and humility.

This powerful truth is set forth plainly in Nephi's testimony: "And it came to pass after I, Nephi, having heard all the words of my father, concerning the things which he saw in a vision, and also the things which he spake by the power of the Holy Ghost, which power he received by faith on the Son of God—and the Son of God was the Messiah who should come—*I, Nephi, was desirous also that I might see, and hear, and know of these things,* by the power of the Holy Ghost, which is *the gift of God unto all those who diligently seek him,* as well in times of old as in the time that he should manifest himself unto the children of men.

"For he is the same yesterday, to-day, and forever; and the way is prepared for all men from the foundation of the world, if it so be that they repent and come unto him.

"For *he that diligently seeketh shall find;* and the mysteries of God shall be unfolded unto them, by the power of the Holy Ghost, as well in these times as in times of old, and as well in times of old as in times to come; wherefore, the course of the Lord is one eternal round" (1 Nephi 10:17–19; emphasis added).

Because our God is no respecter of persons (Acts 10:34; Romans 2:11; Colossians 3:25); because he does not love his prophets and apostles any more than he loves the rank-and-file; because spiritual gifts and the knowledge that comes from them are available to all;

and because the purpose of the gospel of Jesus Christ is to establish a holy society of men and women, all of whom freely "speak in the name of God the Lord, even the Savior of the world" (D&C 1:20), we have the sweet assurance, as did Nephi, that our Heavenly Father can and will reveal himself to one and all, in his own time and according to his own will (D&C 88:68). In the words of the Prophet Joseph Smith, "God hath not revealed anything to Joseph, but what He will make known unto the Twelve, and even the least Saint may know all things as fast as he is able to bear them."[28]

An appreciation for this delightful doctrine is prelude to what follows in the vision. After Nephi explained that he desired to see the things which his father had seen, the Spirit asked what appears to be a most unusual question: "Believest thou that thy father saw the tree of which he hath spoken?" Nephi answered the query: "Yea, thou knowest that I believe all the words of my father" (1 Nephi 11:3–5). One wonders about that question: Why did he not ask Nephi if he believed that his father had seen a large and spacious building, mists of darkness, a strait and narrow path, or a rod of iron? The fact is, the Spirit of the Lord was not simply inquiring into Nephi's knowledge of a form of plant life. Indeed, it was not a belief in the *tree* which would qualify Nephi for the manifestation to follow; nor was this the Spirit's objective. The tree was obviously a symbol, a sign pointing beyond itself to an even greater reality.

The vision enjoyed by Lehi and Nephi is Christ-centered and is to be fully appreciated only by focusing attention upon him who is the author of salvation. Consider the following:

1. After Nephi had certified his belief in the fact that his father saw the tree, the Spirit "cried with a loud voice, saying: Hosanna to the Lord, the most high God; for he is God over all the earth, yea, even above all. And *blessed art thou, Nephi, because thou believest in the Son of the most high God;* wherefore, thou shalt behold the things which thou hast desired" (1 Nephi 11:6). Note that the guide rejoiced over Nephi's *faith in Christ*, not his belief in a tree.

2. The Spirit began to unfold the typology to Nephi. The tree has been given "for a sign" (1 Nephi

11:7), as a symbol of a man, even him whose branches provide sacred shade from the scorching rays of sin and ignorance.

3. The fruit of the tree was white. Whiteness generally symbolizes purity. Jesus of Nazareth was the purest of pure, for he lived without spot or blemish, the only mortal to achieve moral perfection through never wandering from the path of righteousness (2 Corinthians 5:21; Hebrews 4:15; 1 Peter 2:22).

4. After Nephi had been asked concerning his knowledge of the condescension of God and had then seen Mary "carried away in the Spirit for the space of a time," he "looked and beheld the virgin again, bearing a child in her arms" (1 Nephi 11:19–20). Nephi's account continues: "And the angel said unto me: Behold the Lamb of God, yea, even the Son of the Eternal Father! Knowest thou the meaning of the tree which thy father saw?" (1 Nephi 11:21). That is, while looking at the Christ child, it is as if his guide were summing up, bringing Nephi back to the point where he had begun—the deeper significance of the tree. Essentially Nephi was asked, "Now, Nephi, do you finally understand

the meaning of the tree? Now do you understand the message behind the sign?" And he answered: "Yea, *it is the love of God*, which sheddeth itself abroad in the hearts of the children of men; wherefore, it is the most desirable above all things" (1 Nephi 11:22; emphasis added). The angel then added by way of confirmation: "Yea, and the most joyous to the soul" (1 Nephi 11:23). Nephi's answer was perfect: his understanding was given by the power of the Holy Ghost. Again, the tree represented more than a vague (albeit divine) sentiment. It was the greatest manifestation of the love of God—the gift of Christ. "For God so loved the world," Jesus explained to Nicodemus, "that he gave his only begotten Son, that whosoever believeth in him should not perish, but have everlasting life" (John 3:16; compare D&C 34:3). That love is made manifest and is extended to all men through the Atonement—it "*sheddeth* itself abroad in the hearts of the children of men" (1 Nephi 11:22; emphasis added)—through, appropriately, the blood *shed* in Gethsemane and on Golgotha.

There is no limit to the love of the Father that

can be received by all who qualify for salvation. "And again," Moroni spoke to the Savior, "I remember that thou hast said that thou hast loved the world, even unto the laying down of thy life for the world. . . ." Moroni added, "And now I know that this love which thou hast had for the children of men is charity" (Ether 12:33–34).

5. Finally, we attend carefully to Nephi's words regarding the tree: "And it came to pass that I beheld that the rod of iron, which my father had seen, was the word of God, which led to *the fountain of living waters, or to the tree of life;* which waters are a representation of the love of God; and I also beheld that the tree of life was a representation of the love of God" (1 Nephi 11:25; emphasis added). The "fountain of living waters" or "water[s] of life" (Revelation 22:1–2), linked to the tree of life very often in the literature of the ancient Near East,[29] would seem to symbolize the cooling draft available through him alone whose words and works are as an oasis in the desert of the world, indeed, he who is "the fountain of living waters" (Jeremiah 2:13). "Whosoever drinketh of the water that I shall give him shall never thirst," Jesus said to the Samaritan woman, "but the water that I shall give him shall be in him a well of water springing up into everlasting life" (John 4:14).

And so now we have become privy, to some extent at least, to the vision of the tree of life that Nephi and Lehi beheld. We have become partakers of precious truth and sobering realities. This vision is a testament to the goodness and perfect love of God the Father; a reminder that "salvation was, and is, and is to come, in and through the atoning blood of Christ, the Lord Omnipotent" (Mosiah 3:18); and a plea and invitation to all men and women—all of the sons and daughters of God—to exercise judgment, to be true to that inner light that the scriptures call the Light of Christ or Spirit of Jesus Christ, to choose wisely how they will spend their days of probation. "For behold, this life is the time for men to prepare to meet God; yea, behold the day of this life is the day for men to perform their labors" (Alma 34:32). In the poignant words of Jacob, son of Lehi, "O be wise; what can I say more?" (Jacob 6:12).

HOLD TO THE ROD, THE IRON ROD

ARTIST'S NOTES

I have enjoyed the many artistic interpretations of Lehi's dream. It seems that often artists create the dream as one painting, a vast montage that presents every aspect of the vision simultaneously, as if we as viewers are looking at the entire landscape from far away. This approach has always bothered me somewhat, because the dream of Lehi and the subsequent explanation to Nephi were not given as a single picture, but rather as a series of vignettes, or scenes, each observed in its own time frame, so the dream reveals itself more like a motion picture than a painting. Short of illustrating it as a film, I wanted to create a series of paintings that highlighted the significant scenes.

When this project started out, I began studying my own dreams, trying to understand how the images presented themselves. They were not logical, and did not progress seamlessly, but faded and moved and redefined themselves as they went. A character that was not around in scene two was a major player in scene three, and no one in the dream seemed troubled or concerned about his appearance. So it made perfect sense to me that Lehi did not observe and describe everything in every scene. His narrative works, but it unfolds in a dreamlike manner.

As I painted the illustrations for the book, I kept the values dark, highlighting only what Lehi was seeing. When I have worked on films I have been fascinated by the huge dark soundstage, filled with equipment and lights and cables, all in a dim interior. And then, in the middle of the gloom, light! As the actual set for the scene is illuminated and it shines out of the dark stage, our attention is drawn to the light; we pay little attention to what is in the shadowed interior. This is the feeling I wanted to achieve in these paintings.

The scriptures are rich with stories. The history of the ancients, as individuals and groups, give us many insights into the nature of man and God's relationship to his children. These histories help us understand our own times and our own natures. In addition to the historical narratives in the scriptures, we are often taught by parables, visions, and dreams recorded by the writers of our sacred books.

Dreams are given in the scriptures for different reasons. Some dreams are given as riddles to be interpreted by God's prophets and thus establish themselves with the political leadership as divinely inspired men (Joseph in Egypt, Daniel in Babylon). Other dreams are straightforward and are often warnings or prompts to action (Joseph, husband of Mary).

Visions are often "big picture" experiences that individuals are given on rare and sacred occasions. In addition to the visions of Moses and Abraham, we have an example here of the vision of Nephi, who wished to understand the dream of his father. Nephi was shown the whole life and mission of the Savior to help him understand the meaning of the fruit of the Tree of Life. Many of the

Tree of Life, detail.

other symbols in Lehi's dream were explained and illustrated for Nephi in the course of his vision. It is interesting to me that Lehi's dream was very personal and dealt with his family. When Nephi experiences his vision, it becomes much more universal. The tree of life is a powerful image in Lehi's vision, and also a powerful image in art. It shows up in varied cultures around the world and back through time. Because of its universality, I've included small examples of that motif throughout the book.

The Savior often taught in parables, or stories, both to enlighten the prepared minds of his disciples and to confound his adversaries. Because I am a visual thinker, the parables of the Lord offer me a rich field of ideas and images to contemplate and to identify with. It was a delight several years ago to create a book with Robert Millet in which we illustrated, examined, and discussed some of the parables of Jesus. These brief stories teach us in a unique way about ourselves, our duties, our shortcomings and our spiritual potential. Often the same parable has multiple applications. At different times in my life I have identified with the prodigal son, the father, and the older brother. These divinely crafted stories offer us many layers of information and insight. This appeals to me as an artist because I would like my own work to communicate on multiple levels, to continue to feed the viewer over time as he or she contemplates the work.

A friend of mine took a framed print of *Hold to the Rod, the Iron Rod* to a Young Women's class she was teaching. She wanted to teach a lesson on the material versus the spiritual. To her surprise, the visual aid she brought to get the class's attention took over the entire lesson. The girls began examining the objects the little character is clinging to, and then began to make comparisons with their own lives and their physical and spiritual "stuff." This makes me feel good. If my work can inspire ideas or examination, can open eyes to new ways of looking at ourselves and the world, I think I am accomplishing something worthwhile.

As you read this book and consider the imagery, I don't doubt that you will often say, "That's not what the tree looks like, or the great and spacious building!"—but that is part of the magic of art. You won't hurt my feelings if you say that you have always seen it differently. That is the beauty of art. When we read Lehi's dream in the scriptures, each of us can conjure up our own vision of what it looked like. And maybe, if you look at some of the paintings and say, "I never thought of it that way, but this works and helps me understand things in a different way," that makes me happy. I encourage readers to ponder the scriptures that describe and interpret Lehi's dream, Brother Millet's commentary, and the artwork that I have included to find new meaning in, more connections to, and new insights from this beautiful story.

NOTES

1. See also Joseph Smith, *History of the Church*, B. H. Roberts, ed., 7 vols., 2d ed. rev. (Salt Lake City: The Church of Jesus Christ of Latter-day Saints, 1932–51), 3:379.

2. Boyd K. Packer, "Spiritual Crocodiles," *Ensign*, May 1976, 32.

3. Joseph Smith, *History of the Church*, 5:134–35.

4. Neal A. Maxwell, *That My Family Should Partake* (Salt Lake City: Deseret Book, 1974), 1.

5. Maxwell, *That My Family Should Partake*, 3.

6. Joseph F. Smith, *Gospel Doctrine* (Salt Lake City: Deseret Book, 1971), 313.

7. See Ezra Taft Benson, "Beware of Pride," *Ensign*, May 1989, 4–7.

8. Dieter F. Uchtdorf, "Pride and the Priesthood," *Ensign*, November 2010, 56.

9. Jeffrey R. Holland, "Place No More for the Enemy of My Soul," *Ensign*, May 2010, 46.

10. David O. McKay, quoted from J. E. McCulloch, *Home: The Savior of Civilization* (Washington, D. C.: The Southern Co-operative League, 1924), 42; in Conference Report, April 1935, 116.

11. See Harold B. Lee, "Follow the Leadership of the Church," *Ensign*, July 1973, 95–99.

12. "The Iron Rod," *Hymns of The Church of Jesus Christ of Latter-day Saints* (Salt Lake City: The Church of Jesus Christ of Latter-day Saints, 1985), no. 274.

13. See Harold B. Lee, *Ye Are the Light of the World* (Salt Lake City: Deseret Book, 1974), 211.

14. See Wilford Woodruff, *Discourses of Wilford Woodruff* (Salt Lake City: Bookcraft, 1946), 5.

15. *Lectures on Faith* (Salt Lake City: Deseret Book, 1985), 75–76.

16. Bruce R. McConkie, *The Promised Messiah* (Salt Lake City: Deseret Book, 1978), 561.

17. Russell M. Nelson, "A More Excellent Hope," *Ensign*, February 1997, 61.

18. Jeffrey R. Holland, *Christ and the New Covenant* (Salt Lake City: Deseret Book, 1997), 336.

19. Dieter F. Uchtdorf, "The Infinite Power of Hope," *Ensign*, November 2008, 21.

20. *The New Shorter Oxford English Dictionary*, 2 vols. (Oxford: Clarendon Press, 1993), s.v. "disconcert."

21. Harold B. Lee, *Stand Ye in Holy Places* (Salt Lake City: Deseret Book, 1974), 92.

22. Brigham Young, in *Journal of Discourses*, 26 vols. (Liverpool: F. D. Richards & Sons, 1851–86), 16:123.

23. C. S. Lewis, *Letters to Malcolm–Chiefly on Prayer: Reflections on the Intimate Dialogue between Man and God* (New York: Harcourt Brace & Company, 1992), 30.

24. C. S. Lewis, *Mere Christianity* (New York: HarperCollins, 2001), 196–97.

25. Hugh Nibley, *Since Cumorah* (Salt Lake City: Deseret Book, 1967), 393.

26. Bruce R. McConkie, "Jesus Christ and Him Crucified," *1976 BYU Speeches of the Year* (Provo, Utah: BYU Press, 1977), 400–401.

27. Joseph Smith, *History of the Church*, 4:11.

28. Joseph Smith, *History of the Church*, 3:380.

29. See John M. Lundquist, "The Common Temple Ideology of the Ancient Near East," in *The Temple in Antiquity*, ed. Truman G. Madsen (Provo, Utah: BYU Religious Studies Center, 1984), 53–76.

NOTES ON ADDITIONAL ARTWORK

Page 9: Border decorated with a Tree of Life, from Siphnos, Cyclades, 17th–18th century (cotton embroidered with silk threads), Greek School / Benaki Museum, Athens, Greece / The Bridgeman Art Library International

Page 21: Tree Portiere tapestry, made for William Morris & Co., c. 1909, Dearle, John Henry (1860–1932) / Private Collection / Photo © The Maas Gallery, London / The Bridgeman Art Library International

Page 33: Tree of life made of stone in mosque at Ahmedabad, Gujarat, India. Getty Images / Dinodia Photos / Brand X Pictures.

Page 41: Persian rug displaying the tree of life. Getty Images / Massimo Pizzotti / Photographer's Choice RF

ABOUT THE ARTIST

JAMES C. CHRISTENSEN'S award-winning art is prized in collections throughout the U.S. and Europe. He has received numerous professional honors, including his induction into *U.S. Art* magazine's Hall of Fame. He is an Honored Alumnus at Brigham Young University, where he is a frequent guest lecturer. In addition to his fine art paintings, his work is the focus of several acclaimed books, including *Parables* (also with Robert Millet), and a series of interactive journals. He and his wife, Carole, live in Orem, Utah, where he currently serves as a bishop of a singles' ward.

ABOUT THE AUTHOR

ROBERT L. MILLET, former dean of Religious Education at Brigham Young University, is the author of numerous books. He has been the Richard L. Evans Professor of Religious Understanding at BYU and manager of Outreach and Interfaith Relations with the Public Affairs Department of the Church. He currently serves as director of Religious Studies at BYU. He and his wife, Shauna, live in Orem, Utah.